DOGS
IN TRANSLATION
Workbook

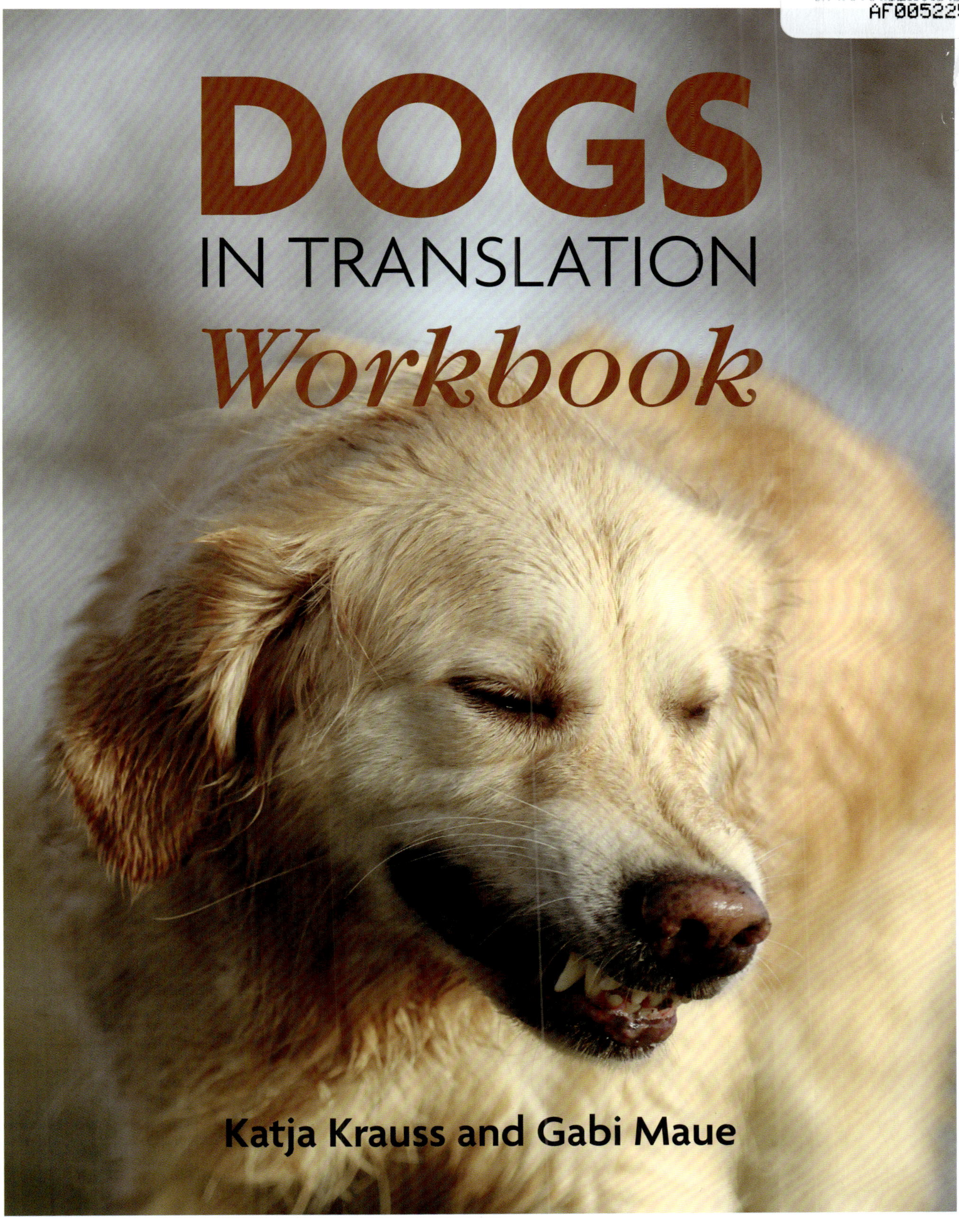

Katja Krauss and Gabi Maue

First published in Germany in 2020 by Kynos Verlag
Copyright 2020 Katya Krauss, Gabi Maue and Kynos Verlag

English language edition published in 2022 by First Stone Publishing,
an imprint of Westline Publishing Limited
The Old Hen House, St Martin's Farm, Zeals, BA12 6NZ, United Kingdom

English Language edition
Copyright 2022 Katya Krauss, Gabi Maue and Westline Publishing Limited
ISBN 9781910488652

All rights reserved. No part of this book may be used or reproduced in any manner whatsoever,
including electronic media or photocopying, without written permission from the publisher.
Printed by Printworks Global Ltd., London & Hong Kong.
1234567890

Photo credit: All photos, including front and back cover: Katja Krauss except:

Gabi Maue: pages 8, 34.
Ingvil Schirling: pages 11 top, 12 middle, 28 top, 38 top, 39, 53 right;
Sophia Wild: pages 28 and 53 left

CONTENTS

INTRODUCTION 4

HOW TO USE THIS BOOK 5

1. WHAT DOES THE DOG'S BODY TELLS US? 6
    1.1. Facial expressions 6
    1.2. The ear 7
    1.3. The eye 8
    1.4. The mouth and wrinkles 9
    1.5. Shifting the point of balance 10
    1.6. The tail 11
    1.7. The coat 12

2. COMMUNICATION SIGNALS 13
    2.1. Blinking 13
    2.2. Tongue flicking 14
    2.3. Head turning 16
    2.4. Walking in an arc 17
    2..5. Cowering 18
    2.6. Sitting down and sniffing 19

3. UNEXPECTED HAPPENINGS 20
I see something you don't see

4. ARE YOU SERIOUS? 22
Fight or play?

5. THE EMOTIONS 23

6. OUTCOMES 30

LAST WORD 52

WHY THIS WORKBOOK?

In our book, *Dogs In Translation*, we featured the wide variety of expressions, communication signals and behaviours which dogs use in different situations. With this workbook, our aim is to help you school your eye so you are able to pick up the important, subtle details that reveal how our dogs feel.

We feature photos or photo sequences, with a short description of the situation, and ask you to describe what you see. We then ask you to answer the questions we have set for each situation. For example: "What do you think will happen next in this situation?" Once you have made your evaluation, you can turn to the end of the book to discover the outcome. We have grouped the exercises so that they correlate to the chapters in The Emotional Life of Dogs. However, you work through them in the order you prefer.

There are no points awarded for getting the answers 'right' or 'wrong'. This is not a competition, it is about creating awareness and fine-tuning your observation skills. Once you know what to look for, you will get better at noticing the most subtle of signals and, with time and experience, you will evaluate situations correctly. Eventually, there will come a time when your understanding becomes instinctive; you will know instantly how a dog is feeling. When that happens, we have achieved our goal!

Katja Krauss and *Gabi Maue*

HOW TO USE THIS BOOK

SAMPLE EXERCISE

Here two dogs are meeting each other for the first time.

Describe, objectively, what you observe from their body language. Concentrate on the black dog:

- Tail carried low
- Neck stretched upwards, head slightly tilted down
- Right ear turned to the back at the base and held flat against the body
- Eyes slightly rounded, eyebrows raised slightly
- Looking straight at the approaching dog
- Mouth closed
- Top of the head tightened
- Clear shift of balance to the back
- Hind legs spread far apart

Question. *How does the black dog feel about the dog that is approaching him from the front? What is likely to happen next?*

OUTCOME

The black dog seems very unsure; he is fearful, almost frozen. He jumps to the side when the approaching dog comes closer. Looking at his body language in the first photo, he could have remained in a frozen stance. It is highly unlikely that he would have initiated an attack. His hind legs are spread far apart, which tells us that he is preparing to flee.

1. THE BODY

1.1. FACIAL EXPRESSIONS

This is Max: A hand is being lowered towards his head from above.

Describe precisely what you see. Make notes, and then answer the question (below).

....
....
....
....
....
....

Questions
1. What is likely to happen when the hand gets closer to Max?
2. How he is feeling in this photo?

Outcome: See page 30

1.2. THE EAR

Robbie, the small brown puppy, would like to play with Spot, who is lying down.

Note down your observations, paying particular attention to both dogs' ears.

....
....
....
....
....
....
....
....
....
....
....
....
....
....
....

Questions
1. How is Spot going to deal with Robbie's advances?
2. Looking at the way both dogs hold their ears, can you work out how they are feeling?

Outcome: See page 31

1. THE BODY

1.3. THE EYES

Here Quivive (left) meets Dora, a female Bavarian Mountain Dog.

First describe Quivive, then Dora, using all three photos. When looking at Quivive pay attention to the backline, the way she carries her tail and where she shifts her weight. When looking at Dora, focus on her face and eyes.

....
....
....
....
....
....
....
....
....
....
....
....
....
....

Questions
1. How does Quivive feel about this interaction?
2. If she is uncomfortable, can you tell what triggered it?

Outcome: See page 32

1.4. MOUTH AND WRINKLES

In these photos we see Ronnie, an adult Golden Retriever, being crowded by Arwen, a young Collie Poodle cross. She is out of shot to the right of Ronnie. She is excited about jumping into the car and almost bumps into him.

Describe what you can see, focusing on the mouth and wrinkles.

....
....
....
....
....
....
....
....
....
....
....
....
....
....
....
....
....

Questions
1. How does Ronnie feel about this situation?
2. How is he likely respond within the next second?

Outcome: See page 33

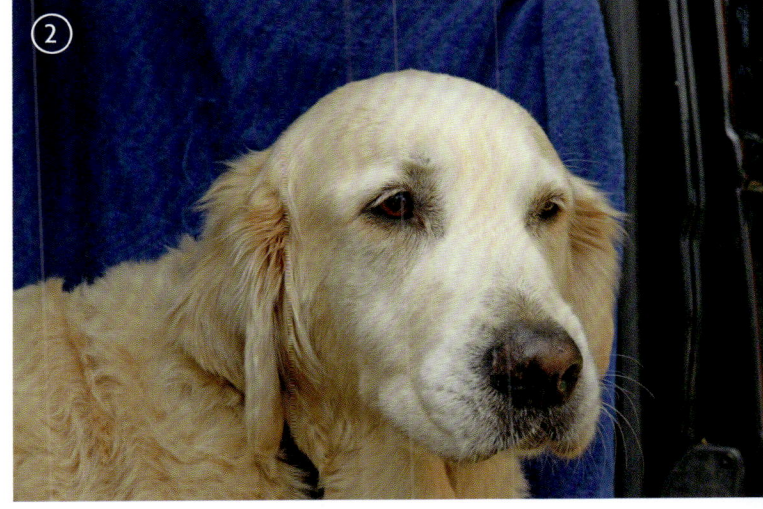

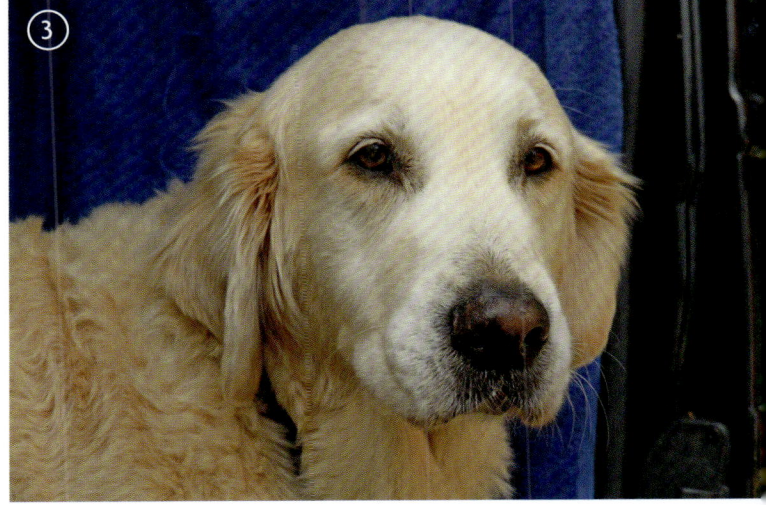

1.5. SHIFTING THE POINT OF BALANCE

Tamika (right) would like to play with Eve, a female Yorkshire Terrier. These two dogs live in the same household and are well acquainted with each other.

Describe Eve and pay extra attention to the way she shifts her point of balance.

....
....
....
....
....
....
....
....
....
....
....
....
....
....
....

Questions
1. Are the dogs going to play?
2. What gives a clue as to what will happen next?

Outcome: see pages 34 and 35

10 Emotions Workbook

1.6. THE TAIL

Neo, an Australian Cattle Dog (left) meets an unfamiliar dog at the beach. Describe everything you see in both dogs. The first photo shows the situation from a different perspective; looking at the tri-colored dog (right) you can see only a tiny portion of his tail positioned by his left hind leg. Note the tail in the following two photos: how does it change between photos 2 and 3?

Questions
1. Can the tail carriage give us clues about how this interaction will develop?
2. What is most likely to happen next?

Outcome: See page 36

1. THE BODY

1.7. THE COAT

These two females do not know each other. They met at a park and engage in a brief interaction.

In the first photo, pay particular attention to the white- and tan dog.

Describe the smaller mixed breed female in the second photo.

The third photo shows what happened next. Describe what you have noticed about the tan-and-white dog's coat.

....
....
....
....
....
....
....
....
....
....
....
....

Question

1. Looking at this interaction, and focusing on the third photo, do you have an explanation for the raised hairs visible on the tan-and-white dog?
Outcome: see page 37

2. COMMUNICATION SIGNALS

2.1. BLINKING

Rani, the Golden Retriever, is chewing on a stick when Neo, the Australian Cattle Dog, joins her. He is also interested in the stick.

Describe, photo by photo, what you see in both dogs. Focus on Neo (left) first, and then Rani (right).

Questions
1. How will Rani respond to the fact that Neo is still interested in 'her' stick.
2. Did Neo influence the outcome of the situation by blinking?

Outcome: See page 38

2.2. TONGUE FLICKING

Here we see typical male posturing, which can often be observed when entire males meet for the first time. Before the first photo was taken, the two dogs had already circled around each other a few times and first one, then the other, urinated.

In the third photo, the males are joined by Rani, a female Golden Retriever. At the time she was staying with the guardian of Chi, the white dog. Looking at these photos, especially the first two, you can see how much easier it is to read white dogs compared to black dogs.

Give a detailed description of what you can see in each photo, in turn, starting with Chi, and then moving on to the black male.

Questions
1. Interpret the mood between the two male dogs in the first two photos. How did this meeting develop?
2. How did the interaction change when Rani joined the males, keeping in mind she knew one of the male dogs?

Outcome: see page 39.

2.3 HEAD TURNING

This puppy sees someone with a camera and large lens for the first time. In addition, he hears the clicking of the shutter.

Describe what you see.

....
....
....
....
....
....
....
....
....
....
....
....
....
....
....

Questions
1. How is this young dog feeling?
2. Why is he using the head turning signal?

Outcome: See page 40.

2.4. WALKING IN AN ARC

This small tan-coloured female was born a street dog, and is very shy towards people. She now lives in a shelter in the Arabian Emirates. Here, the trainer who was working with her that day is trying to coax her to come closer with treats.

Give a detailed description of the tan-coloured dog in all three photos.

Questions
1. Why did the tan-coloured dog walk in an arc?
2. How is she feeling?
3. Did she finally take the treat from the trainer's hand?

Outcome: See page 41

2.5 COWERING

This puppy is also from a street-dog family and was taken to the shelter in the Arabian Emirates. He is still very shy and unsure around people.

Describe in detail what you see in the three photos.

....
....
....
....
....
....
....
....
....
....
....
....
....
....
....

Questions
1. What do you think will happen when the trainer stands up?
2. Which physical and postural clues led you to that conclusion?

Outcome: See page 42

2.6 SITTING DOWN AND SNIFFING

These puppies have just been taken into an arena to play. Marvin (black-and-white) is the youngest and smallest in the group. He has a long line so it's easier to catch him when he's running free. The other puppies think it's fun to pull on the leash.

What can you see in these photos? Describe the body language of the black-and-white puppy.

....
....
....
....
....
....
....
....
....
....
....
....
....
....

Questions
1. Is Marvin going to start playing with the other puppies?
2. How else could he respond?
3. Which body language details were most important in coming to your conclusion?

Outcome: See page 43

3. UNEXPECTED HAPPENINGS

3.1. I SEE SOMETHING YOU DON'T SEE ...

These three dogs just met at the beach; they don't know each other. Describe the body language of the small dog, in the middle, in the first photo. Can you see where he is looking? Are there any signs of tension?

After you have described the first photo in detail, have a look at the next photo. Are there any marked differences between the two? What are the similarities?

Note the changes between the second and third photos.

20   Emotions Workbook

Questions
1. What was the trigger for the small dog's behaviour?
2. Did Tamika, the light-coloured female who was running beside him, influence his behaviour?
3. Did the small dog's facial markings play a part in your assessment? If so, what was the significance?

Outcome: see page 44

4. ARE YOU SERIOUS?

4.1. FIGHT OR PLAY?

Max and Daniel are Golden Retriever siblings from the same litter. They live together and, obviously, know each other well.

Examine the three photos carefully and describe the facial expressions in each.

....
....
....
....
....
....
....
....
....
....
....
....
....

Questions
1. What happens next?
2. What is the mood of both dogs in the last photo?

Outcome: See page 45

Max is pictured left and Daniel is on the right.

This is Daniel.

Again, Max is pictured left and Daniel is on the right.

5. EMOTIONS

5.1. WHICH EMOTIONS DO YOU SEE?

Emotion: ....

Dhanyi (right) shows typical young dog advances towards the adult, Bruno. Dhanyi has known Bruno all her life.

What exactly do you see here? First describe the physical traits you see in Bruno, and then move on to Dhanyi, the female Golden Retriever.

....
....
....
....
....
....
....
....
....
....
....
....
....
....
....

Questions
1. How does the interaction develop between the two photos?
2. Are the dogs still playing, or are they getting serious?

Outcome: see page 46

5.2. WHICH EMOTIONS DO YOU SEE?   Emotion: ....

This is another example of young dog advances. The female Border Terrier, wearing a pink coat, is still very young. During a break in training, she runs up to an adult Golden Retriever.

Look closely at the three photos and give a detailed description of what you observe. First describe the Border Terrier, then the Golden Retriever.

....
....
....
....
....
....
....
....
....
....
....
....
....

Questions
1. What do you think will happen when the Border Terrier gets up?
2. How could these two dogs react?
3. What choices do they have?
4. Which is the most likely, and why?
5. How would you describe how each of these dogs is feeling?

Outcome: See page 47

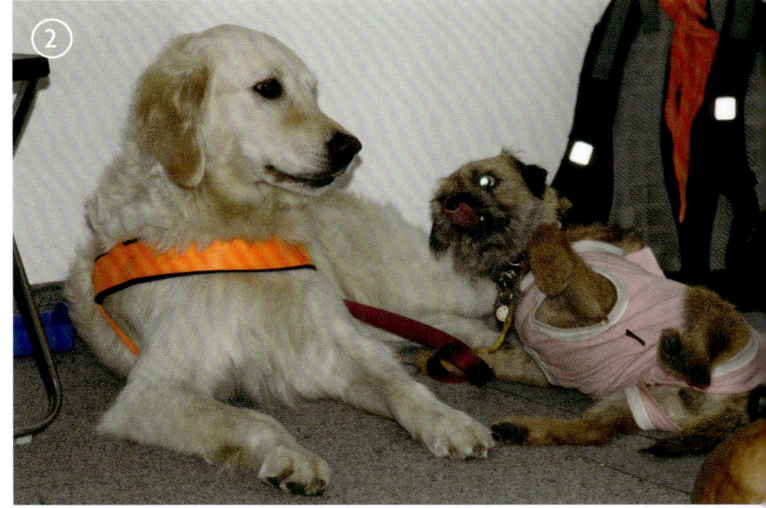

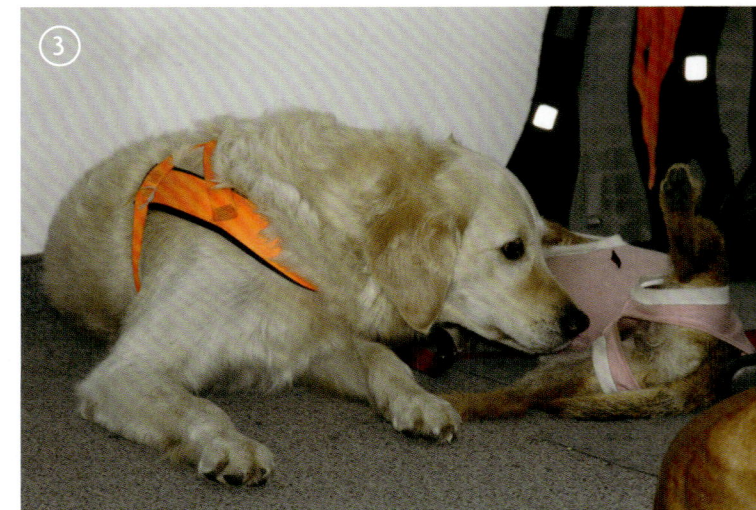

5.3. WHICH EMOTIONS DO YOU SEE?   Emotion: ....

When these photos were taken, Jean, the small, light-coloured dog, had only lived with the other two female dogs for a few weeks. Dhanyi, the Golden Retriever (left) does not like making contact with unfamiliar dogs. However, both dogs are close in age, and playful. Here Jean shows she would like to start a game. The third dog, in the background, is not relevant to this sequence.

Take a look at the light-coloured female, and the Golden Retriever, and describe what you see.

....
....
....
....
....
....
....
....
....
....
....
....
....

Questions
1. Drawing on the information you have been given about the two dogs, and your observations, what do you think happens next?
2. If Dhanyi wants to avoid the situation, what are her options?
3. Which option will she choose?

Outcome: See page 48

5. EMOTIONS   25

5.4. WHICH EMOTIONS DO YOU SEE? Emotion: ....

Neo, the Australian Cattle Dog (left) and Jean, a light-coloured mixed breed female, have only been living in the same household for a short space of time. Both are between one and two years old. Here we can see them playing at the beach.

Describe in detail what you see. Remain objective; do not evaluate or interpret what you see at this stage. First describe Jean (right), then Neo (left).

....
....
....
....
....
....
....
....
....
....
....
....
....
....

Questions
1. How would you identify Jean's behaviour?
2. Is Neo in danger? Should the dog's guardian interfere in this situation?
3. If you think interference is necessary, which physical clues have influenced your decision?

Outcome: See page 49

5.5. WHICH EMOTIONS DO YOU SEE? Emotion: ....

This Labrador is being introduced to a pig – he has never seen one before.

Describe in detail what you see. Is there anything specific that stands out in these photos?

....
....
....
....
....
....
....
....
....
....
....
....
....
....

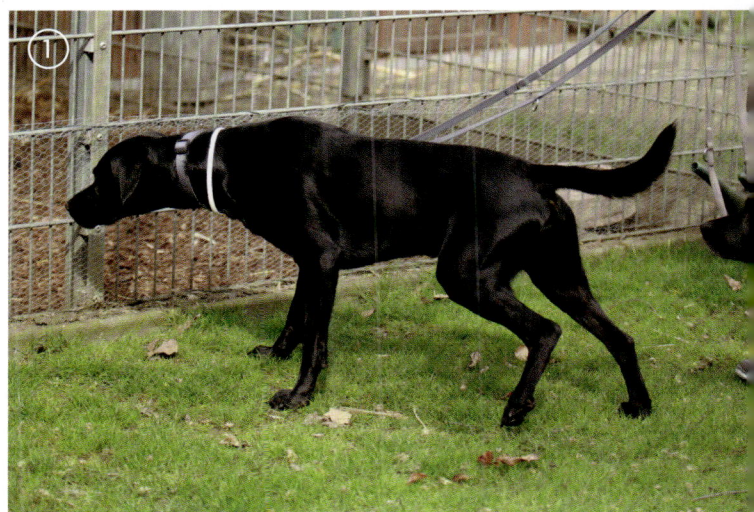

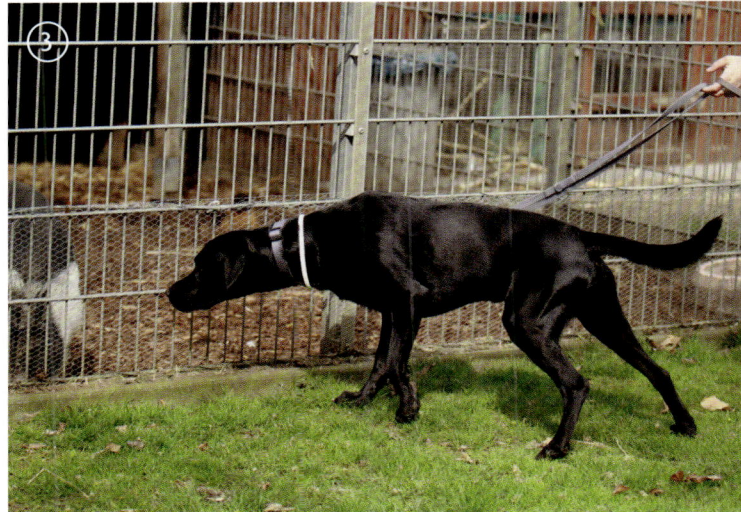

Questions
1. Which emotions are triggered in this dog?
2. What do think will happen next?

Outcome: See page 50

5.6. WHICH EMOTIONS DO YOU SEE?   Emotion: ....

Neo (right, in the first photo) is an entire Australian Cattle Dog. He meets a large mixed breed male, who is also entire, for the first time. The dogs circle each other three times, and the photos show the same situation from different angles. We want to find out if it is important to observe a situation from different angles to make a decision.

Can you spot something new when you see the situation from a different angle? Have you missed an important detail? Was it enough to look at just one photo to make up your mind about the situation?

These two dogs have now circled each other for 24 seconds (in real life that feels like an eternity). The guardian of the mixed breed male has continued walking.

Questions
1. What options do these two dogs have?
2. What do you think will happen next?
3. Which physical characteristics influenced your opinion?

Outcome: see page 51

6. OUTCOMES

1. THE BODY

1.1. FACIAL EXPRESSIONS, page 6

Max, the Golden Retriever: A hand is being lowered towards his head from above.

OBSERVATIONS

Photo 1
- Mouth open, shortened
- Lower canines as well as two back teeth visible
- Tongue relaxed inside the mouth
- Beard hairs pointing forward

Question 1. *What is likely to happen when the hand gets closer to Max?*

Question 2. *How he is feeling in this photo?*

OUTCOME

Max's ears are hanging down loosely. He is smiling and blinks. Sometimes he even shows his teeth when he smiles. His point of balance shows him leaning towards the person. The first photo shows a gesture of belonging which is not so easy to read. The beard hairs pointing forward, the mouth pulled back and the ears flattened and pulled back against the head could be signs of displeasure. However the tongue, sitting loosely in the mouth, contradicts this interpretation. The wrinkles around the mouth indicate stress. However, in this case it is positive stress as Max is very happy to interact with a person he knows.

The follow-up picture shows how much Max enjoys connecting with a person he loves, in this case his osteopath.

1.2. THE EAR, *page 7*

Robbie, the small brown puppy, would like to play with Spot, who is lying down.

OBSERVATIONS

Photo 1: Spot

- Both ears flat against the head and pulled back
- Point of balance to the left while lying down
- Head turned away from Robbie

Photo 1: Robbie

- Hairs raised on the shoulder all the way to the top of the head
- Short tail carried above the level of his back
- Left ear hangs to the side, flopping
- Looking towards Spot
- Mouth open, upper teeth and lower canines visible
- Wrinkles around the nose
- Jumping forward towards Spot with a raised upper body

This is Robbie's natural ear position, which may change as he matures.

Photo 2: Spot
Changes from Photo 1

- Right ear flipped up, head turned away from Robbie
- Mouth wide open, long mouth
- Long tongue, tip of the tongue hangs loosely out of the mouth

Photo 2: Robbie
Changes from Photo 1

- Both ears turned to the outside and upright at the base
- Eyes slightly slit shaped
- Mouth slightly more open, short mouth, lower canines visible
- Upper body less raised while jumping

Photo 3: Spot
Changes from photo 2

- Ears only partially visible
- Point of balance shifted towards Robbie to almost sitting

Photo 3: Robbie
Changes from photo 2

- Left ear upright, turned slightly to the side and down (possibly following his movement)
- Left eye wide open, line of vision and head turned away from Spot
- Mouth longer
- Upper body in the air, shifting point of balance away from Spot

Question 1. *How is Spot going to deal with Robbie's advances?*

Question 2. *Looking at the way both dogs hold their ears, can you work out how they are feeling?*

OUTCOME

This interaction is too much for Spot. Robbie understands and makes himself small. He pulls his ears back at the base. Spot turns away from him.

To work out how the two dogs are feeling, look at Robbie's ears, which are soft and relaxed, and follow the movement of his body and head. Spot's ears can only be seen part of the time, so it's important to evaluate his other body language signals. He is shifting his weight, turning his head and there is little tension in his face.

Overall Spot shows that this is too much for him, but he is not a serious threat to Robbie.

1.3. THE EYES, page 8

Quivive (left) meets a female Bavarian Mountain dog, Dora (right)

OBSERVATIONS

Photo 1: Dora (right)

- Neck slightly raised
- Ears hanging down loosely, lightly raised at the base
- Looking towards Quivive, mouth closed
- Point of balance leaning away from Quivive
- Tail carried lower than the back

Photo 1: Quivive (left)

- Back rounded
- Ears pulled back
- Point of balance leaning away from Dora

Photo 2: Dora

Changes from photo 1

- Hardly any changes

Photo 2: Quivive

Changes from photo 1

- Back straighter
- Neck carried a little lower, head turned away from Dora, looking elsewhere
- Point of balance away from Dora

Photo 3: Dora

Changes from photo 2. The different perspective limits the possibility to compare, but shows previously hidden details.

- Tail level with the back and moving with great amplitude
- Ears raised at the base and held to the side
- Minimal wrinkling above the eyes
- Eyebrows slightly raised, looking towards Quivive, pupil enlarged

Photo 3: Quivive

Changes from photo 2

- Body and head turned away from Dora
- Back rounded
- Tail carried over the back
- Mouth slightly open

Question 1. *How does Quivive feel about this interaction?*

Question 2. *If she is uncomfortable, can you tell what triggered it?*

OUTCOME

Quivive is clearly uncomfortable about meeting Dora, who is too close and engages in direct eye contact.

Even though Dora is reserved and is not being pushy, the intensity of her eye contact is exaggerated by her amber coloured eyes, and the darker markings above them. This leaves Quivive feeling a little unsure.

1.4. THE MOUTH AND WRINKLES, *page 9*

In these photos we see Ronnie, an adult Golden Retriever, being crowded by Arwen, a young Schafpudel. She is out of shot to the right of Ronnie. She is excited about jumping into the car and almost bumps into him.

OBSERVATIONS

Photo 1

- Right ear turned towards the back at the base and pulled tight
- Head turned away from Arwen, top of the head tightened
- Skin below the eyes slightly tensed all the way to the mouth
- Mouth closed, upper lip hanging loosely, beard hairs pointing down

Photo 2
Changes from photo 1
- Neck raised
- Head turned towards Arwen, no direct eye contact
- Start of wrinkles developing around the nose
- Beard hairs raised and pointing forward slightly

Photo 3
Changes from photo 2
- Direct eye contact towards Arwen
- Increased wrinkles around the nose
- Beard hairs clearly pointing forward

Question 1. *How does Ronnie feel about this situation?*
Question 2. *How will he most likely respond in the next second?*

OUTCOME

Ronnie does not feel comfortable because the space around the car door is too narrow. Due to the lack of space, he will escalate his behaviour so he is clearly threatening within the next second.

You can see the subtle escalation of Ronnie's mood in the increased wrinkling around his nose and the direct eye contact. He relaxed within fractions of a second as soon as Arwen passed him. Situations can deteriorate when dogs are forced into close proximity, such as meeting on a narrow path, so this should be avoided whenever possible.

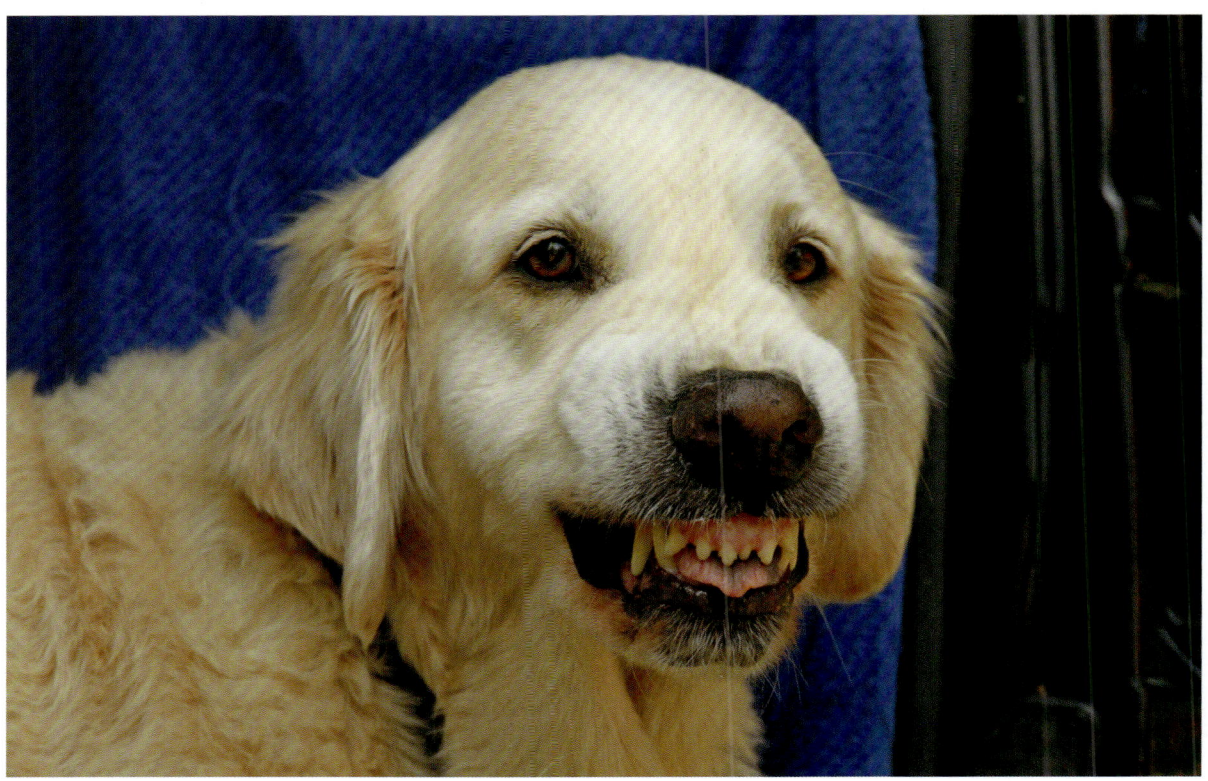

1.5. SHIFTING THE POINT OF BALANCE, *page 10*

Tamika (right) would like to play with Eve, a female Yorkshire Terrier. These two dogs live in the same household and are well acquainted with each.

OBSERVATIONS

Photo 1: Eve (left)

- Tail carried slightly above the level of her back
- Neck raised high, head raised slightly and turned towards Tamika
- Ears held back at the base, no direct eye contact
- Mouth closed
- Standing in balance

Photo 2: Eve

Changes from photo 1

- Back rounded towards the loins, tail held lower than the back
- Neck raised further
- Head pulled back and turned towards Tamika
- Ears pulled far back
- Point of balance shifted towards the back, right front paw lifted

Photo 3: Eve

Changes from photo 2

- Neck raised even further
- Head pulled back further and held as high as possible
- Point of balance shifted even further back, front paws on the ground

34 Emotions Workbook

Question 1. *Are the dogs going to play?*
Question 2. *What gives a clue as to what will happen next?*

OUTCOME
Since Eve doesn't like to play with other dogs, she avoids direct eye contact which could encourage other dogs to approach. By staying motionless and shifting her weight, she makes it clear that she does not wish to interact.

1.6. THE TAIL, *page 11*

Neo, an Australian Cattle Dog, meets an unfamiliar dog at the beach.

OBSERVATIONS

Photo 1: Tri-coloured dog

- Ears slightly raised at the base and held towards the back
- Eyes rather slit shaped
- Mouth closed, upper lip slightly raised
- Tight skin around the muscles of the jaw, beard hairs raised

Photo 2: Tri-coloured dog
From a different perspective

- Back slightly rounded towards the loins, tail carried low
- Head carried higher than back and turned slightly towards Neo
- Ears raised slightly at the base and turned towards the back
- Mouth closed
- Point of balance towards the left and back
- Left front paw raised

Photo 3: Tri-coloured dog:
Changes from photo 2

- Back rounded towards the loins, tail almost clamped
- Head clearly turned towards Neo. Ears almost unchanged
- Point of balance more towards the front while moving backwards simultaneously

Question 1. *Can the tail carriage give us clues about how this interaction will develop?*

Question 2. *What is most likely to happen next?*

OUTCOME

Looking at the tail on its own, you can see the insecurity, or possibly fear, in the tri-coloured dog, but it does not give any clues as to what he is likely to do next.

Both dogs made a dramatic shift in their point of balance (photos 2 and 3). Shifting forward can easily turn into forward action in a dog as tense as the tri-coloured male. However, Neo recognized this instantly and moved sideways to avoid a possible confrontation as the tri-coloured male leapt towards him.

1.7. THE COAT, *page 12*

Two unfamiliar females meet at a park and engage in a brief interaction.

OBSERVATIONS

Photo 1: White-and-tan female

- Back straight
- Neck long, head lowered
- Left ear slightly held to the side and back
- Rounded eye
- Point of balance more towards the front
- Hair over her back is raised

Photo 2: Mixed breed female (right):

- Back lightly rounded
- Neck slightly lowered
- Ears held towards the back
- Point of balance shifted to the side away from the other dog

Photo 3: White-and-tan female

- Hairs raised in the back section of her back

Question 1. *In the third photo you can already see the outcome of the situation. Do you have an explanation for the raised hairs visible on the white-and-tan dog?*

OUTCOME

The three photos show a very relaxed meeting from the white-and-tan female's point of view, while the mixed-breed female shows some concern. The mood created by the two dogs should not cause the raised hairs on the white-and-tan female's back. However, it is not always the immediate situation that is the cause. It may be something that has happened before.

In the photo (below) we see what happened just before the two dogs met. The larger dog (left) sniffed and then took the stick that the white-and-tan female had dropped. The hairs on her back were already raised, most likely because her stick had been stolen. Her excitement and frustration were her predominant emotions when she met the mixed breed female shortly afterwards.

2. COMMUNICATION SIGNALS

2.1. BLINKING, *page 13*

Rani, the Golden Retriever, is chewing on a stick when Neo, the Australian Cattle Dog, joins her. He is also interested in the stick.

OBSERVATIONS

Photo 1: Neo (left):
- Left ear clearly turned towards Rani, right ear just slightly held to the side
- No direct eye contact (whale eye)

Photo 2: Rani (right)
- Back slightly rounded towards the croup, tail tight at the base
- Neck raised, head turned toward Neo
- Ears pulled back and down
- Point of balance toward the back

Photo 2: Neo
Changes from photo 1
- Head clearly turned
- Eyes slit shaped (blinking)

Photo 2: Rani
Changes from photo 1
- Ears slightly more forward
- Posture changed, almost frozen

This is Neo's natural ear carriage.

Photo 3: Neo
Changes from photo 2
- Head dropped low, ears more raised
- Eyes larger, eyebrows raised slightly
- Direct eye contact
- Greater distance to Rani

Photo 3: Rani
Changes from photo 2
- Head and neck slightly lowered
- Back rounded
- Hind legs closer together
- Moving forward, less frozen

Question 1. *How will Rani respond to the fact that Neo is still interested in 'her' stick.*

Question 2. *Did Neo influence the outcome of the situation by blinking?*

OUTCOME

The blinking did not change Rani's posture – maybe the gesture was not clear enough for her?

She can only relax when Neo clearly backs away.

However, when he once again focuses his attention on her, and her stick, she reacts strongly and bares her teeth.

2.2. TONGUE FLICKING, *page 14*

Here we see typical male posturing which can often be observed when entire males meet for the first time.

OBSERVATIONS

Photo 1: Chi (white)
- Tail curled over his back (almost natural tail carriage)
- Neck raised, head slightly lowered, ears pointing forward
- Joints slightly braced

Photo 1: Black male
- Clear tongue flicking
- Head turned away from Chi, not looking at him, ears back
- Tail carried above the level of the back and tight
- Hind legs far behind the body

Photo 2: Chi
Changes from photo 1
- Left ear raised at the base and turned forward
- Looking in the direction of the male dog
- Mouth short, almost closed, tip of the tongue visible
- Skin tightened in the cheek area, beard hairs pointing forward
- Movement in the direction of the other male (left front leg raised)

Photo 2: Black male
Changes from photo 1
- Tail raised a little higher
- Head lowered almost to level of back, ears pulled back
- Whale eye visible on the left – this means the dog is looking forward
- Mouth closed
- Moving away with long strides

Photo 3: Chi
Changes from photo 2
- Head held very low, facing away from Rani
- Right front paw raised

Photo 3: Black male
Changes from photo 2
- Ears in flirt position
- Head lowered slightly, facing Rani
- No direct eye contact between the two
- Tail level with the back
- Left front paw raised (we can't see here if he is standing or walking)

Question 1. *Interpret the mood between the two male dogs in the first two photos. How did this meeting develop?*

Question 2. *How did the interaction change when Rani joined the males, keeping in mind she knew one of the male dogs.*

Chi is quick to stop the black dog making any contact with 'his' female. His mouth is short, and his tongue is deep inside his mouth. It is very clear that his intentions are serious.

2.3. HEAD TURNING, *page 16*

A puppy sees a person with a camera and large lens for the first time. In addition, he hears the clicking of the shutter.

OBSERVATIONS

Photo 1
- Hairs raised in the shoulder area. Tail a little above the level of the back
- Neck slightly raised, head slightly raised
- Ears pulled back at the base
- Eyes large and rounded, looking directly at the camera
- White of the eyes visible
- Joints braced, front and hind legs spread far apart

Photo 2
Changes from photo 1
- Tail dropped to be level with his back and moving
- Head turned, eyes slightly slit shaped
- Mouth closed, puffed cheeks (a sign of stress)
- Left hind leg pointing forward
- Point of balance shifted, moving to the back

Photo 3
Changes from photo 2
- Direct eye contact with the camera, ears pulled further back at the base
- Left hind leg moved back into bracing position

Question 1. *How is this young dog feeling?*
Question 2. *Why is he using the head turning signal?*

OUTCOME

The youngster feels uncomfortable in this situation. By turning his head, he tries to change it. This signal is used to de-escalate and calm.

However, even though he announced his peaceful intentions, the camera that made weird noises and had a huge eye focused on him, did not retreat. The youngster could not leave because he was tied up.

He is very tense and it's difficult for him to stay still, which we can see by the changing movement of his hind legs. He barks to give clues about how uncomfortable he feels, and to release some of his built-up tension.

Note: The visible white in the inside corner of both eyes in an abnormality and may change as he matures.

2.4. WALKING IN AN ARC, *page 17*

The small tan-coloured female was born as a street dog and is very shy with people.

OBSERVATIONS

Photo 1
- Tail carried low, the end is curved upward
- Neck raised a little above the level of the back, head lowered and pointing forward
- Left ear pulled back and touching the head
- Looking straight ahead, mouth closed
- Moving

Photo 2
Changes from photo 1

The white dog has not moved so it is easy to see that the tan-coloured female has walked in a arc.

- Tail lowered
- Head lowered and turned towards the handler
- Eye small, mouth closed, tightened skin around the face
- Continuous movement

Question 1. *Why did the tan-coloured dog walk in an arc?*

Question 2. *How is she feeling?*

Question 3. *Did she finally take the treat from the trainer's hand?*

OUTCOME

Walking in a arc is a typical approach when a dog is unsure, and is also used when being polite. The tan-coloured female was probably a little shy, or felt concerned about the out-stretched hand.

She first walked around the white dog to get closer to the food in the trainer's hand. She then walked in a large arc around the trainer and approached him from the side. Her tightly-clamped tail and pulled-back ears show that she is very tense.

However, the fact that she continues to get closer to the trainer means that she is likely to take the food in the end. The white puppy acts as a buffer and makes her feel a lot safer.

Note the trainer's posture: He is side-on to the tan-coloured dog and crouched down to make himself small. He offers the food with an out-stretched hand, which respects her need for space and makes it easier for her to approach and take the food.

2.5. COWERING, *page 18*

This puppy is also from a street-dog family and was taken to the shelter in the Arab Emirates.

OBSERVATIONS

Photo 1
- Tail close to the body
- Head raised, ears pulled back
- Looking (probably) at the trainer
- Point of balance clearly to the right, sitting

Photo 2
Changes from photo 1
- Point of balance even more to the right
- Right front paw lifted, cowering away from the hand (making himself smaller)

Photo 3
Changes from photo 2

The trainer crouches down so his hand is lower
- Head turned towards the hand, and looking at it
- Licking the hand
- Point of balance shifted clearly more to the right

Question 1. *What do you think will happen when the trainer stands up?*

Question 2. *Which physical and postural clues led you to that conclusion?*

OUTCOME

By making himself smaller, and cowering, the puppy has made it very clear that the hand coming from above – and the resulting contact – is a source of concern.

However, by turning his head towards the trainer and, most likely, looking at him and licking his hand, he shows his indecision. He wants the attention, but the petting makes him feel insecure. As soon as the trainer stands up, the puppy moved away, cowering. He is probably happy to leave.

In these situations, an approach from the side, and touching the dog's shoulder with the back of the hand, would be a more pleasant, and acceptable, experience for the dog.

2.6. SITTING DOWN AND SNIFFING, page 19

These puppies have just been taken into an arena to play. Marvin (black-and-white) is the youngest and smallest in the group.

OBSERVATIONS
Relating to Marvin

Photo 1
- Tail carried very low and tight
- Almost sitting
- Avoiding to the left due to the pull on the leash

Photo 2
Changes from photo 1
- Head turned away from the dog on the left, right ear further back than the left
- Looking over the top and away from the white puppy
- Sitting, point of balance to the right, away from the white puppy

Photo 3
Changes from photo 2
- Tail lowered
- Sniffing

Question 1. *Is Marvin going to start playing with the other puppies?*

Question 2. *How else could he respond?*

Question 3. *Which body language details were most important in coming to your conclusion?*

OUTCOME
Marvin used the communication signals of sitting, and then sniffing, to tell the other puppies that he did not want to play with them. As soon as they lost interest in his long line, he was quick to leave.

3. UNEXPECTED HAPPENINGS
3.1. I SEE SOMETHING YOU DON'T SEE, *page 20*

These three dogs just met at the beach – they don't know each other.

OBSERVATIONS

Relating to the small dog in the middle

Photo 1:

- Tail straight up at the base, curls back to almost touch the back
- Neck raised
- Base of the left ear raised and held to the side, tip of the ear points loosely to the side
- Mouth closed and short
- Slight shift of point of balance to the back, slowing down
- Right front paw raised
- Back rounded towards the loins

Photo 2

Changes from photo 1

- Left ear held towards the back
- Mouth almost closed and a little bit longer, tongue flicking almost invisible
- Right front paw lifted again

Photo 3

Changes from photo 2

- Tail dropped and moving
- Neck raised, head raised and slightly turned towards Tamika (left)
- Left ear pulled back and touching the head. Tip of the ear flies back with the movement
- Mouth open (barking)
- Clearly shifted the point of balance as he is backing up

Question 1: *What was the trigger for the small dog's behaviour?*

Question 2. *Did Tamika, the light-coloured female who was running beside him, influence his behaviour?*

Question 3. *Did the small dog's facial markings play a part in your assessment? If so, what was the significance?*

OUTCOME

Three dogs approached the small dog from the front, which is why he slowed down and shifted his point of balance to the back. His raised neck indicates that he is fully alert to what is happening. He is probably barking because he is startled.

Tamika, the light-coloured female, communicated with him by blinking. The direction of her gaze, and her posture, may have also influenced his behaviour.

The small dog has black markings on the right side of his face, and the change of light creates a shadow. This makes it difficult to evaluate his ears, his right eye and direction of his glance. However, the direction of his nose gives us a good indication of where he is looking.

Here we see, once again, that the first impression is not always correct. Sometimes there are other events happening in the environment that we may have missed, but may influence the dog's reactions.

4. ARE YOU SERIOUS?
4.1. FIGHT OR PLAY? *page 22*

Max and Daniel are Golden Retriever siblings from the same litter. They live together and, obviously, know each other well.

OBSERVATIONS

Photo 1: Max (left)
- Head is beside his brother

Photo 1: Daniel (right)
- Mouth wide open, very few teeth visible
- Beard hairs pointing forward

Photo 2: Daniel
Changes from photo 1
- Ears flying loosely with the movement
- Almond-shaped eyes
- Upper lip hanging loosely
- Shaking off

Photo 3: Max (left)
Changes from photo 2
- Eyes slit shaped
- Mouth wide open and c-shaped with visible teeth (top, front)
- Lower canines – only the tips are visible
- Upper gums visible in the area of the incisors
- Beard hairs pointing forward

Photo 3: Daniel (right)
Changes from photo 2
- Eyes slit shaped
- Mouth wide open and c-shaped
- Upper incisors visible
- Tips of the lower canine teeth visible
- Upper gums clearly visible
- Beard hairs pointing forward

Question 1. *What happens next?*

Question 2. *What is the mood of both dogs in the last photo?*

OUTCOME

After the third photo both dogs ended the game. In the follow-up photo (below), you can see that Max is lying down. Max and Daniel were mouth wrestling, a game that is usually played between dogs who get along well.

However, it does seem that Max, due to his health limitations (extreme joint issues), has made it clear through his facial expressions, that the game was a bit too much for him. The distance between their mouths shows that this was not a serious conflict.

Even littermates who usually get along very well can have individual sensitivities. These can be influenced by external or internal (illness, pain) factors and, as the dogs get older, their interactions may become serious. Therefore, it is advisable to keep an eye on these types of games, even between littermates, and separate the dogs if necessary.

5. EMOTIONS

5.1. WHICH EMOTIONS DO YOU SEE? *Page 23*

Outcome: **Joy**

Dhanyi (right) shows typical young dog advances towards the adult, Bruno. Dhanyi has known Bruno all her life.

OBSERVATIONS

Photo 1: Bruno
- Tail carried above the level of the back, in movement
- Neck raised, head slightly dropped
- Right ear pulled back at the base
- No direct eye contact
- Right front paw on Dhanyi's left shoulder
- Hind legs far apart (to stabilise)

Photo 1: Dhanyi
- Back rounded towards the hind end
- Tail carried slightly below the level of the back, wagging eagerly
- Ears pulled back at the base
- Point of balance towards the hind end
- Joints of the front limbs braced, left front paw raised

Here you can see how the game developed.

Photo 2: Bruno
Changes from photo 1
- Right ear hangs down loosely
- Dhanyi's mouth is in his mouth
- Point of balance towards the hind end

Picture 2: Dhanyi
Changes from photo 1
- Mouth in Bruno's mouth

Question 1. *How does the interaction develop between the two photos?*

Question 2. *Are the dogs still playing, or are they getting serious?*

OUTCOME

During her early years, Dhanyi always licked the corners of Bruno's mouth and even tried to lick the inside of his mouth. This is an expression of the joy she feels when she sees and plays with Bruno. For both dogs this is a pleasurable interaction.

5.2. WHICH EMOTIONS DO YOU SEE? *Page 24*

This is another example of young dog advances. The female Border Terrier, wearing a pink coat, is still very young. During a break in training, she runs up to an adult Golden Retriever.

OBSERVATIONS

Photo 1: Border Terrier

- Cowering, tongue flicking
- Looking towards the Golden Retriever
- Point of balance shifted to the front and right

Photo 2: Golden Retriever

- Neck long
- Head turned slightly and raised, mouth open, mouth short
- Upper incisors, canines and lower canines visible
- Strong wrinkling on top of the nose
- Head turned away from the Border Terrier, ears hanging to the side
- Lying down

Photo 2: Border Terrier
Changes from photo 1

- Lying on her right side, left front and hind paws raised
- Tail between her hind legs

Photo 2: Golden Retriever
Changes from photo 1

- Mouth almost closed, upper lip still slightly raised
- No direct eye contact (despite the whale eye)

Photo 3: Border Terrier
Changes from photo 2

- Lying completely on her right side, left hind leg raised even more
- Tail close to the body and on the ground

Photo 3: Golden Retriever
Changes from photo 2

- Head reaches towards the female's genital region.

In this 'after' photo, you can see (not too clearly) that right after getting up, the young Border Terrier had to shake off her stress. The Golden Retriever used the opportunity to remove himself from the situation. It is also possible that their guardian intervened and encouraged both dogs to get up.

Outcome: **Joy and anger**

Question 1. *What do you think will happen when the Border Terrier gets up?*
Question 2. *How could these two dogs react?*
Question 3. *What choices do they have?*
Question 4. *Which is the most likely, and why?*
Question 5. *How would you describe how each of these dogs is feeling?*

OUTCOME

The young Border Terrier is being very pushy. The Golden is lying close to the wall, so even if he wanted to, he could not move back. Therefore, the Golden Retriever threatens. When the Border Terrier lay down on her side and showed her genital region in response, the older dog relaxed and showed interest in the younger dog.

Both dogs were tense, but in different moods. While the Border Terrier was excited and joyful, the Golden Retriever was angered by her lack of respect for his space. Then he clearly relaxed. The scene could have turned ugly, but when the young dog lay down, the older dog was able to calm himself, and the situation de-escalated.

5.3. WHICH EMOTIONS DO YOU SEE? *Page 25*

When these photos were taken, Jean, the small, light-coloured dog, had only lived with the other two female dogs for a few weeks.

Outcome: **Anger**

OBSERVATIONS

Photo 1: Jean (mixed breed female)
- Tail slightly above the level of her back
- Neck raised slightly, head turned towards Dhanyi (left), slightly raised
- Mouth wide open (barking), lower row of teeth visible
- Left ear loosely to the side
- In movement

Photo 1: Dhanyi (in the foreground)
- Neck raised, head turned away from Jean, slightly lowered
- Ears pulled back, flat
- Right eye, whale eye towards Jean
- Mouth open, lower teeth visible to the corner of the mouth
- Tongue visible, slightly over top of the teeth
- Strong wrinkling around the corners of the mouth

Photo 2: Jean
Changes from photo 1
- Tail raised
- Neck more raised, head turned towards the right
- Ears slightly raised at the base and turned to the front
- Looking straight ahead
- Mouth only slightly open
- Standing

Photo 2: Dhanyi
Changes from photo 1
- Tail slightly lowered
- Neck more raised, head slightly raised
- Ears pointing forward
- Looking straight ahead
- Mouth almost closed

Picture 3: Jean
Changes from photo 2
- Ears flying (upwards)
- Looking at Dhanyi
- Mouth closed
- Galloping after Dhanyi

Photo 3: Dhanyi
Changes from photo 2
- Tail level with the back
- Head turned slightly towards Jean
- Dhanyi leaves, trotting

Question 1. *Drawing on the information you have been given about the two dogs, and your observations, what do you think happens next?*

Question 2. *If Dhanyi wants to avoid the situation, what are her options?*

Question 3. *Which option will she choose?*

OUTCOME

Dhanyi, the Golden Retriever, is clearly annoyed by Jean's on-going requests to play. She has tried to use her facial expression (eyes) and posture to tell Jean that she is not interested in a game.

As this has not worked, she spins round and barks at Jean. You can see the degree of her anger by the tension around her mouth, the forward pointing beard hairs and raised hairs on her back.

If Dhanyi had agreed to play, she could have avoided the confrontation.

5.4. WHICH EMOTIONS DO YOU SEE? *Page 26*

Neo, the Australian Cattle Dog (left) and Jean, a light-coloured mixed breed female, have only been living in the same household for a short space of time. Both are between one and two years old. They are pictured playing on the beach.

OBSERVATIONS

Photo 1: Jean
- Head turned towards Neo, slightly raised
- Ears flying high
- Eyes large and round, eye contact with Neo
- Mouth open, upper and lower rows of teeth visible
- Running parallel to Neo, galloping

Photo 1: Neo
- Head pointing straight ahead
- Ears slightly back at the base and turned to the side
- Eye contact with Jean (whale eye)
- Mouth open, bottom right canine and first few molars visible
- Trotting beside Jean

Photo 2: Jean
Changes from photo 1
- Tail carried very high
- Upper and lower gums visible
- Movements towards Neo

Photo 2: Neo
Changes from photo 1
- Head turned away and slightly raised
- Looking away from Jean (whale eye)
- Mouth more open

Photo 3: Jean
- Mouth extremely wide open, gums visible, mouth c-shaped
- Upper teeth touching Neo's left shoulder
- Left ear flying back
- Looking towards Neo

Photo 3: Neo
- Left eye almost closed
- Corners of the mouth pointing up

Outcome: **Joy**

Question 1. *How would you describe Jean's behaviour?*
Question 2. *Is Neo in danger? Should the dog's guardian interfere in this situation?*
Question 3. *If you think interference is necessary, which physical clues have influenced your decision?*

OUTCOME

Neo shows clearly that he is not in any danger. In photo 3, he smiles, even though it looks like Jean is about to eat him. He loves to play and is a complete optimist; he is confident that nothing bad will happen to him.

If Neo had shown any signs of concern, or being threatened, it would have been advisable to call the dogs and separate them for a little while.

In the 'after' photo, you can see that the two dogs continued their game.

5.5. WHICH EMOTIONS DO YOU SEE? *Page 27*

This Labrador is being introduced to a pig – he has never seen one before.

OBSERVATIONS

Photo 1
- Body stretched long in the approach
- Ears held to the side, head and neck raised
- Tail carried level with the back

Photo 2
Changes from photo 1
- Left front paw lifted
- Tail raised
- Hind legs far apart and braced

Photo 3
Changes from photo 2
- Neck lowered
- Forward movement is restricted to the front legs

Outcome: **Fear and curiosity**

Question 1. *Which emotions are triggered in this dog?*
Question 2. *What do think will happen next?*

OUTCOME

Curiosity is the overriding emotion because the Labrador wants to work out what this weird animal could be. However, he is showing signs of fear that make him act cautiously. His state of indecision is evident by his out-stretched body. His nose is reaching forward to investigate the pig, but his hind legs are as far back as possible so he is ready to flee. In photo 3, he has only moved his front feet forward, so he seems ever longer.

As you can see in the 'after' photo, the Labrador decided it was safer to retreat. He is looking for his handler to protect him.

5.6. WHICH EMOTIONS DO YOU SEE? *Page 28*

The male dance: Seen from three different perspectives.

Photo 1: Neo (right)
- Tail can only be imagined (carried low)
- Hind legs far apart

Photo 2: Seen from three perspectives – A., B. and C.

A. Dark male (left)
- Tail very high above the back
- Looking over the top of Neo
- Left hind leg raised

B. Neo (left)
This photo was taken a split second after photo 1
- Front and hind legs wider apart
- Point of balance shifted to the left and back
- Tail lowered, seems tight
- Ears turned to the outside
- Head slightly above the level of his back

C. Dark male (right)
- Body curved towards Neo
- Looking over the top of Neo
- Right front paw slightly lifted
- Wrinkles in the cheek area
- Mouth closed
- Left ear raised and turned towards the front
- Tail carried in an arch over the top

Photo 3: Neo (right)
This photo was taken a split second after photo 2
- Head turned towards the other male (he was not visible in photo 2)

Outcome: **Rage**

- Joints seem braced
- Hind legs far apart
- Point of balance shifted to the left

Photo 3: Dark male (left)
- Spine curled towards Neo
- Left front paw raised
- Looking over the top of Neo

Question 1. What options do these two dogs have?

Question 2. What do you think will happen next?

Question 3. Which physical characteristics influenced your opinion?

OUTCOME

When looking at photo 1, we noticed that it was the only one that showed Neo moving towards the other male. Without this photo, from this precise perspective, the biggest clue that predicted the outcome of the situation would have remained hidden.

It can be illuminating to look at a situation from different perspectives. However, in the majority of cases, seeing the dog from only one perspective is enough to predict the outcome of any given situation.

In this 'after' photo, taken from the same perspective as photo 3, you can see that Neo took a tiny step in the direction of the other male (best seen in the right hind leg). This was the final straw.

This photo shows the next step. Both dogs should be recalled before the situation escalates further.

LAST WORD
AND WHAT IS THE DOG ON THE COVER ACTUALLY DOING?

Rani just finished sniffing and it seems that something got inside her nose.

This caused her to sneeze, which creates an interesting expression on her face.

Rani recovers from the sneeze, creating a lot of wrinkles on her muzzle.

The last photo shows Rani lying down, relaxing on the grass.